# The Sleeping Sickness

Written by
Jill Atkins

Illustrated by
Jen Khatun



Published in 2026 by
**Norwood House Press**
2544 Clinton Street
Buffalo, NY 14224



Printed in the United States of America
Library of Congress Cataloging-in-Publication Data:
Names: Atkins, Jill (Children's author). | Rickard, Stephen, 1957-, author. | Khatun, Jen, illustrator.
Title: The sleeping sickness / written by Jill Atkins, illustrated by Jen Khatun. How to stay alive / written by Stephen Rickard. A Clutch of Cobblers / written by Stephen Rickard.
Description: Buffalo, NY : Norwood House Press, 2026. | Series: Phonics all-stars: phase 5a
Identifiers: ISBN 9781978579019 (pbk.) | ISBN 9781978579026 (library bound) | ISBN 9781978579033 (ebook)
Subjects: LCSH: Reading–Phonetic method–Juvenile fiction. | English language–Phonetics–Juvenile fiction. | Sleep–Juvenile fiction. | Survival–Juvenile fiction. | Vocabulary–Juvenile fiction.
Classification: LCC LB1573.3 A796 2026 | DDC 372.465–dc23

CPSIA compliance information: Batch #CW26NHP: For further information contact Norwood House Press at 1-800-237-9932.

# May 1st

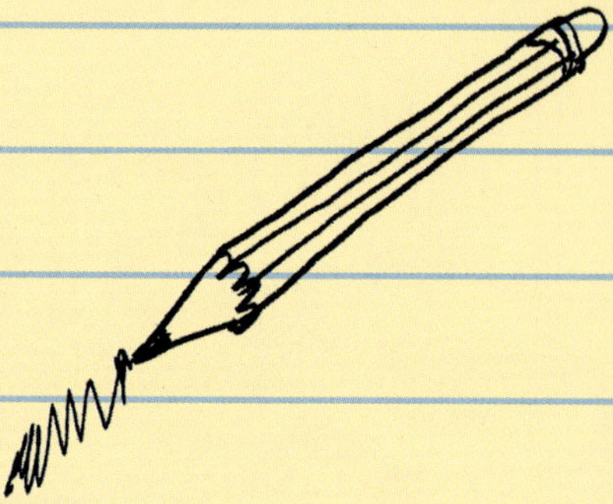

Odd things are happening.

I am starting this notebook so I can jot them down and not forget.

Today, fifteen kids in my grade were late. Fifteen!

They all said they slept late.

Did they get a telling off from my teacher?

No – she had slept in too!

(We didn't snitch on her.)

What is going on?

## May 8th

Just this week:

I have slept in and been late for things.

The number of people sleeping late keeps getting bigger.

The streets are clear at night. No one is out and about.

Coffee is out of stock in all shops.

My friend Mitch thinks I'm paranoid, but this is not normal.

Something is up with people's sleep.

# May 19th

I was right! It said on the news that we are all sleeping longer.

The newscaster said, "All is well." (He was yawning when he said it!)

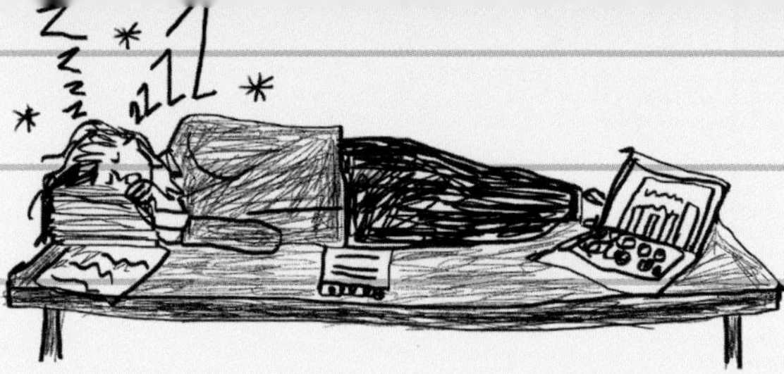

He said that clever people are looking into the problem. And he said that it's not an illness, so we cannot catch it.

Is that good news?

## May 27th

All is not well.

Mitch and I did the math. If people's sleep keeps getting longer like this, then one day ...

(I will not say it out loud, but I am getting a bit frantic.)

## June 8th

Things I have tried, to see if they can keep me awake for longer:

- songs on loud
- lots of sweets
- keeping the lights on all night

No joy yet.

# June 17th

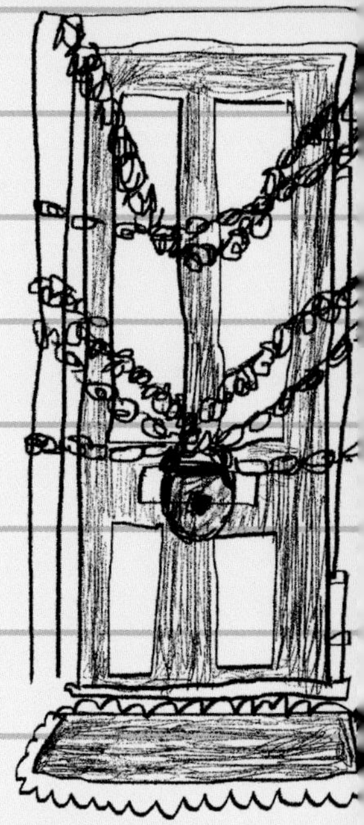

Dad wants us to stay inside.

He said some people are ditching "law and order."

Mom said that those people are "just afraid."

Inside is not too boring, given that the days are so short now.

June 22nd

I woke up at noon. It is now 1PM.

I am in the kitchen, but I feel like I need to crawl back into bed and go back to sleep.

I hear about people dropping off in the street, or on the bus.

When it happens, it is so sudden.

June 30th

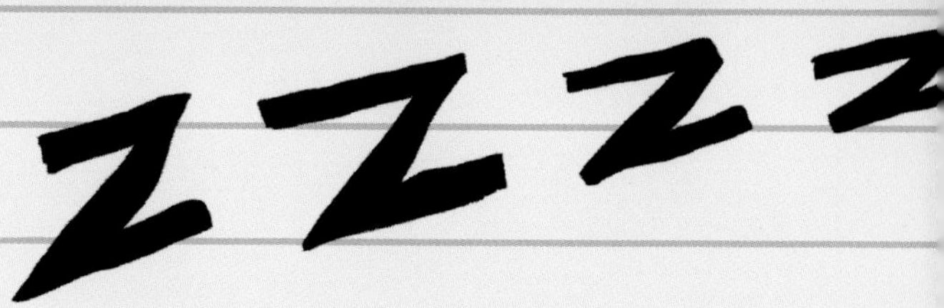

I do not have long to get this down.

It just said on the news that they have found a cure for this "sleeping sickness."

With the days so short now, it will take time to get it to all of us.

But it is good that help is on the w

# How to Stay Alive

By Stephen Rickard

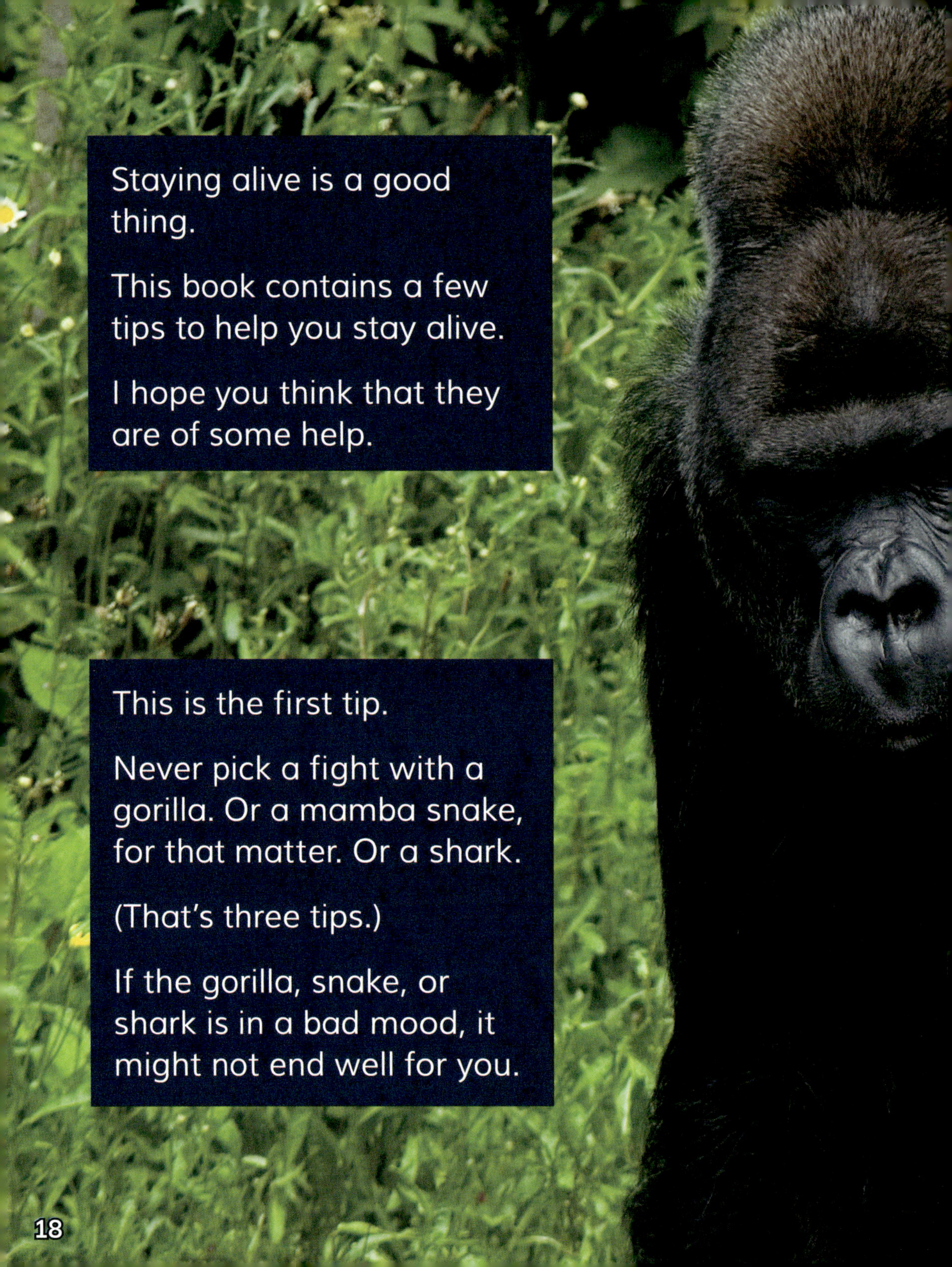

Staying alive is a good thing.

This book contains a few tips to help you stay alive.

I hope you think that they are of some help.

This is the first tip.

Never pick a fight with a gorilla. Or a mamba snake, for that matter. Or a shark.

(That's three tips.)

If the gorilla, snake, or shark is in a bad mood, it might not end well for you.

Never attempt to shoot the rapids in a barrel.

In 1920, a man tried to do this. He strapped his feet to an anvil, then he lay the anvil in the barrel and jumped inside.

However, there was a hitch and it did not end well.

The anvil broke the bottom of the barrel and dragged him down into the river ...

Never go swimming in chain mail. It will not go well.

In 1190, an important lord went for a swim dressed like this.

He drowned.

The lord with his children

Do you have a belt? If you do, never get it trapped in an animal's antlers.

Basil the First did this in 886. He was dragged into the woods for 16 miles.

Then he died.

(What is it about important people and foolish mishaps?)

Basil the First

Do you have a beard?

If you do – never trip on it.

In 1567, a man called Hans Staininger tripped on his beard. He broke his neck and died.

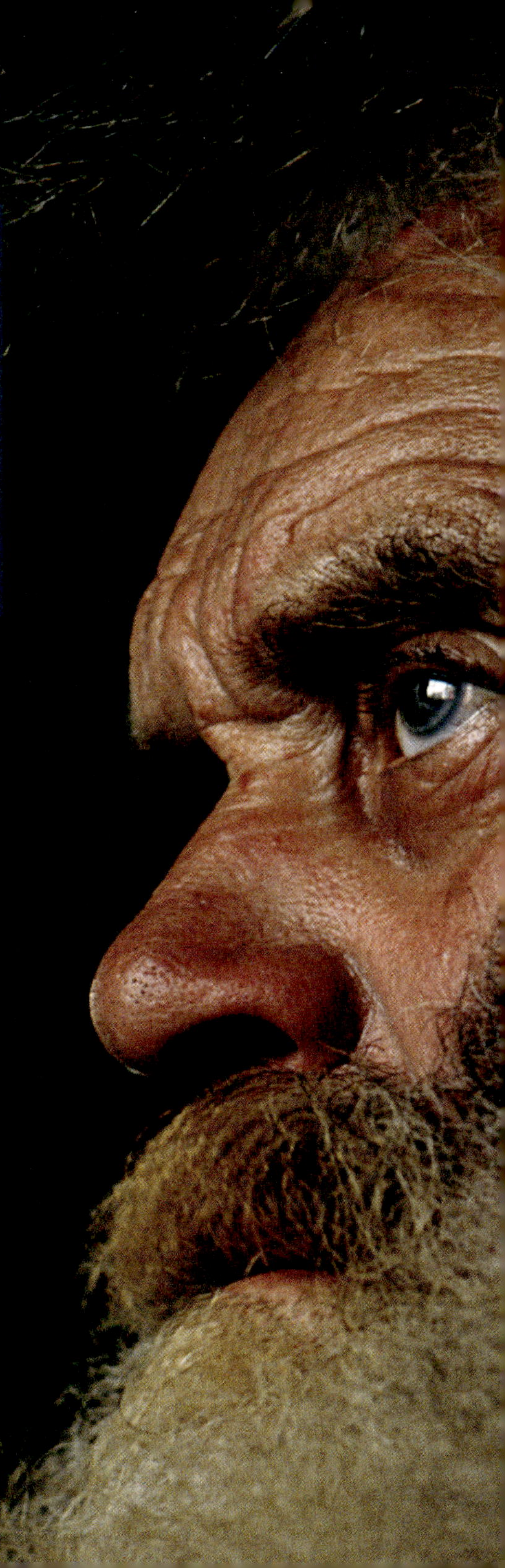

His beard was longer than 4 feet.

As a rule, he kept his beard in a pouch – but not this time. So the lesson is, never ditch the pouch!

Never tie a rock to an alarm clock.

A man did this in 1885. He fixed a ten-pound rock to his alarm clock, so that he'd wake up at the right time without fail.

When the alarm went off, the rock fell on him and killed him.

How about this one?

Never land on a turnip.

In 1881, a British lord (in fact he was a baronet) was out in the woods when he fell on a turnip.

He died.

Do you have some practical tips that you can add?

This might get you started.

# A Clutch of Cobblers

By Stephen Rickard

We have all sorts of names for a number of animals or things.

We often say that there is a fleet of ships, or a flock of sheep.

Have you ever considered these names?

How is it that we never say a flock of ships, or a fleet of sheep?

What are the rules?

Sometimes, it's not hard to understand the reasons for the names.

We say a bunch of grapes. Well, grapes come in bunches, so that's clear.

A flight of birds is fine too. That's what birds do.

A pile of trash? Well, trash piles up, so that's correct.

These are evident too:

- a hive of bees
- a cloud of insects
- a gang of robbers

Sometimes we use the same names.

So it can be a litter of pups, kittens, or fox cubs, but then we say a pack of dogs, a clowder of cats, and a skulk of foxes.

What about chickens? We say it's a brood, or a peep, of chickens.

Then, if it's little chicks, we say it's a clutch.

Ducks are a bit harder. We often say a flock of ducks, but when they are on the ground we can say a badling of ducks.

Then, when they are swimming, we switch to saying a paddling, or a team, of ducks.

Pack gets used a lot.

You can have a pack of dogs, or rats, mules, stoats, and weasels, as well as a pack of cards and a pack of lies.

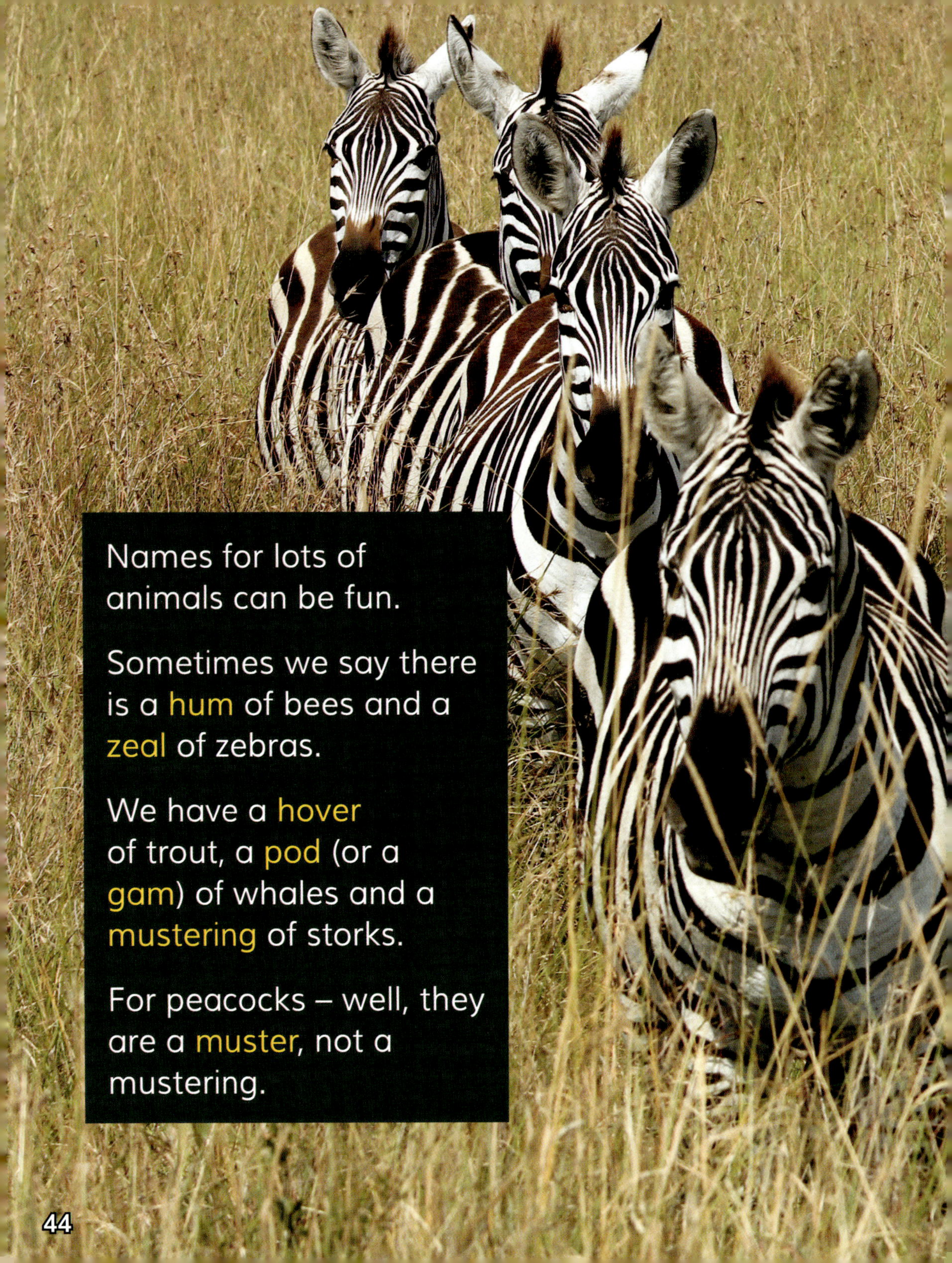

Names for lots of animals can be fun.

Sometimes we say there is a hum of bees and a zeal of zebras.

We have a hover of trout, a pod (or a gam) of whales and a mustering of storks.

For peacocks – well, they are a muster, not a mustering.

For skunks, it has to be a stench. Yes, we say a stench of skunks!

As for kangaroos, we say it is a troop or a mob. I like "a mob of kangaroos" best.

You might not be on top of these names. Some of them are quite odd:

- a groan of puns
- a shrewdness of apes
- a tittering of magpies

These are odd too:

- a romp of otters
- a peck of Frenchmen
- a charm of finches

Do magpies titter? Are finches charming?

Can you think up some absurd names for a bunch of things all together?

Might you say a mingling of moles, or a clump of ditches?

What about a clutch of cobblers? Is that one true?

No. I'm afraid I made that one up.